COMMUNITY DEVELOPMENT

Theory and Practice

Dr. Peter Kibet

Synopsis

This e-book provides students of community education and economic development with a theoretical and practical introduction to this field of study. It provides both a conceptual background and contemporary approaches. The book is divided into four sections. These are community education, community development, community mobilization and community participation.

About the author

Dr. Peter Kibet is a lecturer at Machakos University Department of Early Childhood Education where he teaches courses in reading, language arts and developmental psychology for undergraduate, masters and PhD students. Previously, Kibet taught at Kenyatta University, Mt. Kenya University and Ndalat High School. He has 23 years experience teaching in high school and University. He has published widely in referred journals.

Table of content

Contents

Table of content iii
    CHAPTER ONE 1
    1.0 Introduction 1
1.2 Principles of Community Education 2
Community education is based on the following principles: 2
1.3 Importance of Community Education 3
CHAPTER TWO 5
COMMUNITY DEVELOPMENT 5
    2.0 Introduction 5
    2.1 Community Development 5
    2.2 Background of Community Development Programmes 6
    2.3 Background & Works Of Paulo Freire 6
    2.4 Freire's Principles of Community Education and Development 8
CHAPTER THREE 10
COMMUNITY PARTICIPATION AND CAPACITY BUILDING 10
    3.0 Introduction 10
        3.1.1 Objectives of Community Participation 10
        3.1.2 Factors that facilitate Community participation 10
    3.2 Prerequisites for Optimum Participation 11
    3.3 Capacity Building 12
3.5 Participatory Approaches 13

3.6 Types and Levels of Participation.. 13

3.7 Participatory Rural Appraisal (PRA) 13

3.8 Beneficiary Assessment (BA)... 14

CHAPTER FOUR.. 16

COMMUNITY MOBILIZATION 16

4.0 Introduction... 16

4.2 Skills for Community Mobilization 16

4.3 Community Entry to Exit.. 17

4.6 Challenges of Community Mobilization... 19

4.7 Needs Assessment... 20

4.8 Needs Prioritization 21

References.. 21

About the author

Dr. Peter Kibet is a lecturer at Machakos University Department of Early Childhood Education where he teaches courses in reading, language arts and developmental psychology for undergraduate, masters and PhD students. Previously, Kibet taught at Kenyatta University, Mt. Kenya University and Ndalat High School. He has 23 years experience teaching in high school and University. He has published widely in referred journals.

Acknowledgement

My heartfelt thanks go to Machakos University students who taught me as I taught them and my son Brian who type parts of this e-book.

CHAPTER ONE

COMMUNITY EDUCATION

1.0 Introduction

Let us first define the term community. The term community is used to describe a group of people who though with diverse characteristics are linked by some social ties. The group may share some common perspectives and may engage in joint actions, in the same or different geographical locations. The term community may be based on core elements that include location, elements of sharing, common action, some social or cultural ties and diversity. This means that although the group of people has some links there is an element of heterogeneity.

1.1 Community Education

Community education is a process whereby learning is used for both individual and community betterment. Further, community education may be defined as a process of personal and community transformation, empowerment, challenge, social change and collective responsiveness. The field of community education is about providing the knowledge and skills for people to not only be self-sufficient and independent, but to create and utilize the interdependencies that must also exist in the society. It empowers people to identify, realize and manage their resources effectively and wisely. Through its philosophy and holistic approach, community education builds the capacity of groups to engage in developing a social teaching and learning process that is creative, participative and needs-based. Community education seeks to create a participatory learning culture that incorporates principles and practices of respect, mutual aid, inclusiveness, lifelong learning, skill building, self-appreciation, entrepreneurship, and leadership development.

Community education seeks to build linkages and ensures that the mission is about sustaining communities through education and learning. It reaches out to and engages groups that are not supported by formal education institutions or who would benefit from training and other learning opportunities. It is a vibrant and ever-changing field, unique and interdependent, adapting to the needs of communities by responding with programs specifically tailored to a specific area. Community education is based on principles of justice, equality and inclusiveness. Community education is creative, flexible, dynamic, inclusive, **empowering** and could also be challenging.

1.2 Principles of Community Education

Principles of Community Education

- **Self Determination** – Local people have a right and a responsibility to be involved in determining community needs and identifying community resources.
- **Self Help** – People are best served when their capacity to help themselves is encouraged and developed.
- **Leadership Development** – Training of local leaders in such skills as problem solving, decision making and group process.
- **Localization** – Services, programs and other community involvement opportunities are in locations of easy public access.

Community education is based on the following principles:

1. **Self-determination**: Community members understand their situation hence are better placed to recognize what is most appropriate for them. Parents as their children's first teachers, have a right and a duty to be largely involved in their children's educational matters.
2. **Self-help**: The most suitable way to serve people is to nurture their capacity to help themselves. People gain self-reliance instead of dependence, when they accept ever-increasing responsibility.
3. **Leadership Development:** The identification, development, and use of the leadership capacities of local citizens are prerequisites for ongoing self-help and community improvement efforts.
4. **Localization**: Services, programs, events, and other community involvement opportunities that are brought closest to where people live have the greatest potential for a high level of public participation. Ideally, these activities should be decentralized to locations where the community members can easily access them.
5. **Integrated Delivery of Services**: Organizations and agencies that operate for the good of a community can use their limited resources, meet their own goals, and better serve the public by establishing close working relationships with other organizations and agencies focusing on related purposes.
6. **Maximum Use of Resources**: The physical, financial, and human resources of every community should be interconnected and exhaustively utilized in order to meet the diverse needs and interests of the community.
7. **Inclusiveness:** Community programs, activities, and services, should involve the broadest possible cross section of community residents irrespective of age, gender, religious, ethnic, social, economic or any other differences.
8. **Responsiveness:** Programs and services should respond to the continually changing needs and interests of the community members.
9. **Lifelong Learning**: Learning begins at birth or earlier and continues until death. Formal, non-formal and informal learning opportunities should be available to community members of all ages in a wide variety of community settings.

1.3 Importance of Community Education

Through its political agenda and social purpose, community education challenges outdated norms, structures, values and supports critical reflection. It also empowers besides enabling community members to play an influential role in shaping their lives. A large number of persons in extremely needy situations or area can be effectively reached through community education. Community education is the best way of learning and teaching nonhierarchical situation.

Importance of Community Education
- Encourages active participation by clients
- Encourages clients to be informed consumers
- Encourages higher compliance rates
- Promotes good health and wellness activities

For development in a community, the members need community education. Community education should target all people irrespective of any differences. Human beings are social and interdependent. Consequently, educational decay in a member of a community adversely affects others. Other aspects that make community education important include: -

1. It liberates people from dependency syndrome.
2. It increases ability for people to act as part of a united community for improved living.
3. It provides learning opportunities that address the needs of the community and the individual while ensuring that the learners' experiences are recognized, valued and used as part of the learning process.
4. It nurtures the wellbeing of the participants and their community.
5. It creates a collaborative and creative learning experience that facilitates and supports learners' involvement.
6. It empowers the group focused on to put into practice and perpetuate both locally and nationally, the values of community education.
7. It supports the empowerment of people to identify specific actions needed with regard to their issues and understanding of the reason why collective action should be taken.
8. It encourages community members to critically analyze their existing political, social and economic structures.

1.4 Challenges that require Community Education

There are some challenges that can only be solved through community education. Such include: -

1. Rapid population growth: - Often people think about raising the number of children they can be able to feed. Hardly do some people think about the infrastructure and the public

facilities available. This means that if one family is well-planned and the others in the neighborhood are not, there will be competition for the few resources and thus maims children's optimum performance. This means that community members need to be enlightened on issues pertaining to family planning.
2. Economic disparities: - The gap between the rich and poor can only be reduced through community education. In many Kenyan communities the poor are subdued to such an extent that they adore the rich. Some poor people will spend a whole day discussing the rich. Even when exploited they consider it an opportunity to work with them. Such people need community education to help them out of their helplessness and work towards self-actualization.
3. Environmental degradation: - This is exploitation of available resources due to deforestation, inappropriate waste disposal, soil erosion and air pollution. Community members continue to mess with their natural environment oblivious of the consequences. For proper regulation of seasons there must be trees in a vast environment. This calls for all members' participation. Hazards such as air pollution directly affect the entire neighborhoods indiscriminately. This means that a member who does not get involved in polluting the environment will also be affected by activities of others.
4. Politics: - When there is scramble for power, members of a community require empowerment in order to make wise choices. In Kenya politics, ethnicity has always been misused due to ignorance of the masses. There is need for members of the community to have an exposure of the actual values that they should seek for in an aspiring politician.
5. Conflict: - Conflicts often occur due to ignorance. There is need to provide community education to warring communities in order to help them solve their problems without causing unnecessary harm to others most of whom are often blameless.
6. Marginalized population: - These could be internally displaced persons (IDPs) or refugees from other countries. IDPs are not internationally recognized, thus their needs may not be externally met or addressed. These people need community education to help them become aware of ways in which they could participate for effective living.
7. Epidemics: - When there is an outbreak of an infectious or a contagious disease, community members require education on how to prevent the spread of a disease or how to take care of their affected kinsmen
8. Urbanization: - Since independence, there has been the tendency of rural-urban migration. Most of the migrants move from rural to urban areas in search for employment. They need awareness on how they could utilize the locally available resources for their livelihood.
9. Harmful traditional practices: - Community education is necessary to create awareness on the dangers associated with some traditional practices. This helps the community members to avoid some of the self-instigated problems that the community members often find themselves in. Community education prevents the members from excommunicating or sidelining those who shun the harmful practices.

CHAPTER TWO

COMMUNITY DEVELOPMENT

2.0 Introduction

Like other terms we have come across earlier, Community Development does not have a simple definition because advancement in communities varies according to their specific needs and status. This means that what may be described as development in one community might not be considered as any advancement in another. For example, in one community using handcarts for transport could be considered as development while in another development means transporting goods by air. Nevertheless, Community Development may be described as a process that involves community participation in critically identifying and analyzing their needs, prioritizing those needs, setting goals and making decisions for suitable use of available resources to improve the quality of their lives.

2.1 Community Development

Community Development aims at empowering communities, strengthening their capacities and motivating them towards positive change of attitudes. Community Development approaches try to create self-reliance for self-sustaining development. In addition, Community Development operates within the following principles:

1. Active participation of people in matters that touch their lives
2. Empowerment of community members who are customarily dispossessed of power and control over their community affairs.
3. Involvement of all members of society in the process of social change.
4. Sharing of skills, power, experience and knowledge.
5. Inclusion of neighborhoods and interested communities, in identification of what is relevant to them.
6. A collective process that enhances integrity, skills, knowledge and experience.
7. Empowering individuals and communities to develop and change at their own pace, according to their own needs and priorities.

2.2 Background of Community Development Programmes

Historically, human beings have always worked together to promote their welfare. Consequently, human beings have evolved from stone-age to hunting and gathering, and to the modern agriculture and industrialized development. Community development as a paradigm is prompted by the emerging needs of a people and the pressure to cope with the global technological advancement.

The history of Formal community development programs can be traced from 1930s. The formal welfare programs were geared towards poverty relieve in urban areas in USA and Britain. In African countries, formal development programs in the form of the social welfare program begun after the 2nd world war. The British colonial officers used the principles of community development to prepare the African communities for social-economic development. The Africans over-relied on foreign aid, and the withdrawal of the aid in 1960 when attention shifted to green revolution movement, the socio-economic development programs suffered a lot.

The Green Revolution Movement focused on the enhancement of the agricultural program by providing farmers with improved seeds, fertilizers, machines and other technological renovations. Poor farmers could not afford the input and as such never benefited from the movement. This led to failure of Green Revolution Movement and prompted re-emergence of Community Development Strategies. These included two approaches namely:

1. Basic Needs Approach. This approach sought to ensure that the basic needs of the majority poor were met
2. Rural Integrated Development. ` This sought to holistically address the problem of rural poverty

The two strategies emphasized on community members' participation for community development. In the 1980s, it was found necessary to empower the community members to participate in their own development. This was based on the fact that outsiders do not transfer technology but they share methods which local people can utilize in their own context. The principles of community development can be used to address problems of poverty and under-development

2.3 Background & Works Of Paulo Freire

One of the major personalities who have played a major role in community education and development strategies was Paulo Freire. In order to understand the reasons behind Paulo Freire's contribution in community development it is necessary to look into his background.

In 1921, Freire was born in a middle-class economic family in Brazil. In1929 Brazil was hit by serious economic depression and Freire's family was not spared. The family moved to a lowly city where life could be manageable. Freire spent his social life with peer poor children, from whom he learned a lot. The economic situation exposed him to poverty and hunger that negatively impacted on his ability to learn to the extent that Freire ended up four grades behind.

Finally, their family's misfortunes turned around greatly improving their prospects. The painful experiences molded Freire's concerns for poor people and aided him to construct specific educational viewpoint in which he dedicated his life to improving poor people's lives. Freire enrolled at Law School and also studied philosophy. Although he did law, he never practiced law but instead taught as a teacher in secondary schools.

He realized that the people who were depressed needed self-awareness. This led him to begin his work on the basis of setting the poor free in an attempt to create a new world.

In 1946, Freire was selected as Director of the Department of Education and Culture of the Social Service in one Brazilian state. In this capacity he worked mainly among the illiterate and poor people. In 1962 he applied his theories of teaching among 300 illiterate sugarcane farmers who learned ability to read and write in just 45 days. This made the government to embrace his methodology.

In 1964, the Brazilian government was overthrown in a military coup and Freire's approach was mistaken for an underground movement. As a result, Freire was arrested and jailed for 70 days. Afterwards, he moved to Chile as apolitical exile. There he introduced his method and within 5 years it became widespread.

He was invited as a visiting professor to Harvard University, United States of America, where he taught at the Center for Studies in Education and Development. During this era, Freire wrote his best renowned work, *Pedagogy of the Oppressed*, in which he considered to raise individuals' consciousness of oppression and transform oppressive social structures through community education.

In 1970, Freire left Harvard and went to Geneva, where he worked as assistant secretary of education for the World Council of Churches in Switzerland for a period of ten years. The position provided him an opportunity to travel around the world helping countries develop literacy reforms.

After fifteen years of exile, Freire went back to Brazil after an invitation from the government. There he commenced an institute that meant to bring scholars and critics of his pedagogy into "a permanent dialogue that would nurture the advancement of new educational theories and concrete interventions in reality. He came up with a number of principles that continue to positively impact on community education and development.

2.4 Freire's Principles of Community Education and Development

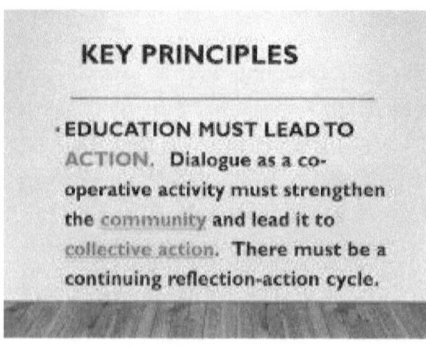

KEY PRINCIPLES

- EDUCATION MUST LEAD TO ACTION. Dialogue as a co-operative activity must strengthen the community and lead it to collective action. There must be a continuing reflection-action cycle.

1) **No education is ever neutral**
   This means that education results to something. It may encourage maintenance of an existing situation or trigger the need to change for the better. This implies that community education empowers people to assess their behavior in relation to the ideal situation. An individual who has been doing the right thing continues without some form of self-doubt. One who has been ignorant acquires a skill, knowledge or new values. This means that education sets people free thus facilitates room for creativity and creative thinking. It further creates awareness and liberates people from ignorance.

2) **Community education must be relevant**
   This means that the topic for community education must be chosen in relation to the context of a particular community. People normally take action or become interested when they have strong feelings about a topic or project. In community education and mobilization, topics or projects should be chosen in relation to identification of gaps. This is in line with the bottom-up approach that emphasizes the importance of incorporating ordinary people's ideas in projects meant for them. A community educator should ideally focus on ordinary people before consulting with the leaders.

3) **Community education poses a problem**
   Freire called problem posing education prophetic. This is because this kind of education seeks to avert undesirable situation before it takes it becomes unmanageable. Community education also seeks to equip people with ideas on strategies that they could embark on to solve an identified problem. Problem posing education helps people to understand more clearly who they are, where they have come from and where they are, so that they can approach the future more wisely.

4) **Community education should be a mutual learning process**
   The agent of change or animator must encourage participation of community members. Freire argues that the animator must have humility, coupled with love and respect for the community members. Humility enables one to listen even to those considered less competent. This is based on the fact that no-one knows it all and no one is ignorant of everything. This means that we all know something and at the same time we are all ignorant of something. This further implies that everyone can make some meaningful contribution without which full success may not be realized. Hence, in community education, everyone is either a teacher or a learner at some point.

5) Community education should involve reflection and action

   Members of the community should be allowed to critically reflect on their situation and to think of ways in which existing gaps could be filled. When members of a community reflect critically on what they are doing, identifying new training and planning, they start addressing their issues. The first plan of action may solve some aspects of the problem, however, it may not fully tackle the main causes of the problem. This means that there is need to set up regular reflection and action sessions where the group celebrates their success, critically evaluates mistakes and failures. This helps the community members to become more skilled and focused. Ideally, community education should lead community members to yearn for more information. The most appropriate type of community education follows a pattern of actions that involves stopping, looking thinking and changing.

6) Community education should lead to radical transformation

   This emphasizes the transformation of the whole world and the fact that everyone has a role to play. This is based on the knowledge that improvement of the world requires the joint effort of all community members.

2.5 Freire stressed the following points:
   i) Getting community members actively involved.
   ii) Breaking through apathy, a state in which people are not interested.
   iii) Developing critical awareness of the roots of a problem: Freire says that the mobilization process is based on insights into different levels of consciousness and the relationship between emotions and motivation to act.
   iv) The use of bottom-up approach in choice of topics/projects as opposed top-down approach. It is necessary to note that people in a community are the experts of their own problems.

CHAPTER THREE
COMMUNITY PARTICIPATION AND CAPACITY BUILDING

3.0 Introduction

Community Participation is a continuous process in which a community organizes itself and takes responsibility for managing its problems. Taking responsibility includes identifying the problems, developing actions, putting them into place, and following through.

3.1 Community Participation

3.1.1 Objectives of Community Participation

i. Identifying problems, needs and other important values
ii. Providing critical information related to the problem
iii. Generating ideas to solve the existing problems
iv. Evaluating alternatives and pick the best option
v. Resolving conflict by consensus
vi. Providing feedback and facilitating continuous action

3.1.2 Factors that facilitate Community participation

i. Conducting consultations where the people are;
ii. Working with traditional leaders, and the full range of community groups and organizations;
iii. Ensuring that the scope of consultation is appropriate to the decision being made;
iv. Limiting the number of management and consultative bodies to which communities have to relate;
v. Giving communities and other interested parties adequate, intelligible information and enough time to consider it, contribute to proposals themselves and respond to invitations to consult;
vi. Ensuring that consultations are in a culturally acceptable form. For example, indigenous people with a tradition of decision-making by communal discussion should not be expected to respond with a written submission from one representative. The indigenous consultation mechanisms that may exist should be used.

vii. Ensuring that the timing of consultations is right. This means that consultation should not take place so early that no useful information is available, or so late that, all people can do, is react or oppose detailed proposals.

3.2 Prerequisites for Optimum Participation

To facilitate community members optimum participation in projects, there are some conditions that must be focused on. Such include autonomous organizations and homogenous membership.

Autonomous organization
i. Membership: This should include the community members at the grassroots. Such organizations counterbalance the larger uncontrollable power concentration at the higher levels and also strengthens the small community members' collective capacity for self-defense. These organizations need support from development agencies but caution must be taken to ensure that the community does not over rely on such agencies. The agencies should ideally empower the community to collectively bargain for their position and to have their collective voice heard.
ii. Leadership: Such organizations are managed by the community members themselves. The leaders must be properly oriented to ensure their motivation and commitment.
iii. Organizational structure: The members should be allowed to participate in decision-making in the group operations as opposed to rigid and bureautic structures.

2. Homogenous membership.
    i. Importance of homogeneity: For authentic representation of common interest and avoidance of conflicts in interests, homogeneity must be considered. In many cases people with similar problems naturally get into some kind of grouping either for consolation or to seek a way out. Homogeneity prevents domination by some members and facilitates effective participation.
    ii. Social differentiation and economic stratification: It is not easy to get a completely homogenous community. This means that there is need for narrowing down the criterion for homogeneity. This could be based on either vertical social differentiation or horizontal stratification.
    iii. Vertical differentiation
    This includes cultural, ethnic or gender status. These factors cut across the layers. There may be concerns that affect a group that has such ties and members would work towards common solutions.
    iv. Horizontal stratification
    This includes economic classes. Though the criteria may vary from one community to another, these classes can be established through wealth ranking exercises.

3.3 Capacity Building

Capacity building refers to a endless process of strengthening stakeholders' ability and capability to determine their individual priorities and values and to consolidate themselves to take suitable action based on the priorities. Capacity building aims to create skills and experience, rise opportunities and boost involvement in decisions that affect community members. It seeks to optimize utilization of resources and opportunities.

This process involves identifying existing capacity resources and assessing the gaps that exist to implement community mobilization. The gaps identified should be supplemented by capacity building of the community groups and other relevant stakeholders involved in community mobilization. Community capacity building, as both a concept and a strategy, has relevance to all communities and to society as a whole. It is, however, most commonly applied to disadvantaged communities.

The ideas behind community capacity building are not new and many of the aspirations, processes and strategies of community development are entrenched in the current manifestations of community capacity building.

3.4 Some Underlying Values

The capacity building approach is based on the understanding that certain groups and communities have been, or are in danger of being 'left behind' in the society and that they need to 'catch up'. In this view capacity building clearly endorses the value of equal opportunity and social equity.

In its emphasis on participation and a more collaborative approach between different sectors, capacity building reinforces the value of participatory democracy and also expands the meaning of democratic governance at all levels. The concept of capacity *building* is also based on the conviction that all communities – regardless of their status have strengths or resources. This apparently simple and self-evident understanding contradicts the 'deficit' prism through which disadvantaged people and communities are usually viewed.

While the main purpose of capacity building in a community is often to achieve a specific outcome, it is argued that capacity building is also a desirable end in itself because it contributes to the creation and maintenance of communities' active involvement. Community capacity building can be viewed as both a process and an outcome or as both a method of working and a value in itself. Considering the complexities of the concept, capacity building contains some internal tensions and ambiguities. These include:

- There are not always local solutions to local problems, regardless of the strength of a community's 'capacity'. Some problems require national level changes in policies, political approaches or resource allocations.
- The 'community' is not a homogenous entity. Within any community there are different viewpoints and interests. These may prompt some occasional conflicts.
- There can be significant inconsistencies between the goals and desired outcomes set by government and those preferred by local community organizations. In this view it is not clear who best reflects 'the community's wishes' (government bodies or local

organizations), and should there always be shared decision-making and a search for consensus between the community
- The community leaders are not necessarily the representatives of the community or democratically appointed and thus may have other interests. It should be understood that, only motivated and willing individuals move things forward and make change happen.

3.5 Participatory Approaches

Participatory approach is a practice where community members are invited to cooperate with the agents of change, researchers and developers, during the several stages in the course of a project or programme innovation. The members participate during the initial exploration and problem definition and pool their ideas together in search for a solution. During implementation, they help evaluate proposed solutions.

The participatory approach in community development becomes effective when it utilizes principles of self-help, felt needs and participation. When members of a community display high levels of felt needs, they are very likely to think of problems as relevant and a priority for instituting change. The notion of cross-cultural variability calls for extensive investigations to develop a body of knowledge concerning the problems facing a particular community prior to the implementation of programme/project for some intended change.

Community Developers are supposed to exploit participatory methods so as to gain insight into local community's strengths and weaknesses. This is because knowledge of problems is connected with actions required and that solutions are produced by community stakeholders who are beneficiaries of change.

3.6 Types and Levels of Participation

There are many different types of participatory approaches that can be utilized to help a community to define their needs. These include: -

3.7 Participatory Rural Appraisal (PRA)

This is refers to the methods employed by Non- Governmental Organizations and other agencies involved in international development. PRA developed in late eighties in South – India, Nepal and Kenya. PRA sought to bring extra people-centered approach to the development practice by laying emphasis on community members' active role in pursuing their own agenda and having more power in decision making process since they are bound to understand their situations better than anyone else. The PRA approach seeks to incorporate the knowledge and opinions of rural people in the planning and management of development projects and programmes.

This approach was in contrast to the prevalent practice of the donors and aid workers who had the main power in deciding about how communities should be assisted. Within several years from its inception, PRA became widely used by NGOs, academics, governments and communities. One of the reasons of such popularity has been its methods which, include **and empower people in matters that affect their lives.**

Self-esteem, Associative strength, Resourcefulness, Action planning, Responsibility (SARAR)

This is an education/training methodology for working with stakeholders at different levels to engage their creative capacities in planning, problem solving and evaluation. The five attributes and capacities in this approach are considered the minimum essentials for participation approach to be a dynamic and self-sustaining process. The attributes are described as follows: -

i. Self-esteem: a sense of self-worth as a person as well as a valuable resource for development. Community members only feel free to participate when they know that they are appreciated for who they are.
ii. Associative strength: the capacity to define and work toward a common vision through mutual respect, trust, and collaborative effort.
iii. Resourcefulness: the capacity to visualize new solutions to problems even against the odds, and the willingness to be challenged and take risks.
iv. Action planning: combining critical thinking and creativity to come up with new, effective and reality-based plans in which each participant has a useful and fulfilling role.

Responsibility: Ability to follow-through until the commitments made are fully discharged and the hoped-for benefits achieved.

SARAR is based on the principle of fostering attributes among the stakeholders involved in the evaluation. Such a process enhances the quality of participation among all the stakeholders.

3.8 Beneficiary Assessment (BA)

Beneficiary Assessment is refers to qualitative method of collecting information on beneficiary perceptions toward an activity. *The method is described as involving participant observation and intensive qualitative interviewing in the project communities by professionals trained to develop information attuned to the needs of local project management.* By using focus groups, semi-structured interview and observations, information can be collected, measured and tabulated to show how stakeholders will value improvement.

Community groups having more power are likely to be engaged and previously have had their voice and perspective heard. Because of economic and cultural differences some communities have less power. This shows that a number of participatory methods should be purposefully be employed in a community to come up with solutions that embrace all stakeholders.

In any participatory approach, it is important to consider matters appertaining to accountability. Accountability plays an important role in making sure that there is maintenance of steady relationships amongst the different stakeholders. It is important to make the leaders of the project accountable to community members, who are the beneficiaries. This makes the community members have courage to get involved and be committed to the success of the project and project's sustainability.

For the project's success it is important to assist community members cultivate a sense of its ownership. If community members get involved in the process of decision making, they cultivate a sense of project ownership. Generally, project sustainability depends on the level of community ownership members feel they have in the project. Without the participation of the local community, projects often fail. Ideally, there should be interdependence between the local community and the external agents of change.

The first step in the evaluation of participatory approaches is to look at social and cultural customs of the society. It is largely believed that the finest way of promoting community participation is by inspiring community to own and to take part in projects meant for their community development. The need for self-reliance must also be considered since without it participants may continually rely on the project without concern for development.

CHAPTER FOUR

COMMUNITY MOBILIZATION

4.0 Introduction

Community mobilization is defined as a procedure through which a collection of people has gone past their own personal differences to converge on equivalent terms so as to enable a participatory decision-making practice. Community mobilization can also be defined as a process that starts a dialogue amongst community members so as to decide who, what, and how issues are decided. It also offers an avenue for everybody to take part in the decisions and activities affecting human lives.

4.1 Community Mobilization

WHY COMMUNITY MOBILIZATION IS NECESSARY

- Prevention and control of diseases requires the co-operation and participation of the community.
- In order to make the community aware of the benefits of disease prevention and control and the role they can play.
- Community mobilization helps to decrease or reduce mobility from diseases in the community.
- Members of the community may have ideas or resources to improve disease prevention and control.

A sense of immobility may be prompted by factors such as:

1. The misconceptions that some other persons will help curb the problems a community experience.
2. Ignorance and lack of skills among the community members.
3. Community members not willing to abandon personal interests for the sake of community development.
4. Scarcity of resources needed to help process of mobilization.

4.2 Skills for Community Mobilization

To be able to mobilize a community, the animator must be competent in the relevant skills. The agent of change should: -

i) Have appropriate skills for communication
ii) Help people to be free to express themselves and to diagnose their needs together with respect for each other. This helps community members to become better able to analyze their problems.
iii) Help community members to plan, pool their resources together and to act together in terms of organization.

iv) Have ability to create rapport with the community members. This influences acceptability.
v) Have ability to facilitate an affirming atmosphere that helps members to develop confidence and participate consistently.

4.3 Community Entry to Exit

When entering a community, one must be careful to ensure that he or she wins the community members' support. It is important to note that:

- The first step is to identify in each situation who are co-operating and plan how to get them actively involved
- There is need to plan a campaign of awareness for the apathetic or passive group. The campaign will aim at encouraging them to agree and co-operate, as they get more and better informed on the facts.
- The opposition group will need to be engaged in constant dialogue both as a group as well as individuals. If dialogue does not succeed, some form of social pressure may be considered. No violence should be involved at any time under whatever circumstances. This would be a sign of weakness. Courts of law should be used where necessary. Legal redress is a sign of social maturity, responsibility and integrity.

4.4 Factors to Be Considered for Effectiveness
- Avoid the temptation of doing for the people what they can do for themselves.
- Gather facts for sharing information to as many people as possible. Understand the views of the opponents to be able to counter effectively with facts.
- After public meetings follow-up with cluster groups for deeper analysis of the situation.
- Use peers to win over their friends: youth to youth, elders to elders, women to women professionals to professionals.
- Take counsel from the views of opinion leaders but be aware of attempts to manipulate you. In other words, be critical but politely so.
- Take care when you ask for permission. Sometimes it is enough to inform. Otherwise, should permission be denied, you are demobilized with no option left.
- Be friendly to all in order to win trust and confidence, hence be open.
- Understand people's reality, as well as their fears and limitations to be able to see through their eyes and speak in their 'language" the more you appeal directly to their hearts and not just to their intellect.
- Make clear the end benefits of the sacrifices you are calling them to make.
- Appeal to both reason and emotions, by using eloquent speakers, role plays, drama, stories and music.
- Never accept 'no' for an answer easily; do not give up too early
- Where possible advice members of your team to behave unpredictably towards the opponents. For instance, co-operate with the opposition when they least expect it . Such as attending their meetings when they invite you, and being friendly even when they scorn you.
- Where possible accept compromise without betraying your team of co-operators.
- Seek to forge large networks and alliances of support, both internal and external.

4.5 The Basic Steps of Community Mobilization

The following are the steps that should be followed while mobilizing a community: -
i) Reconnaissance visits: initial casual visits for casual contacts, followed by semi-formal introductions to the local structures. More formal visits follow for familiarization and initial dialogue and consultations. This is also the opportunity to get to know the community, and make contacts with formal and informal organizations.

ii) Negotiations: This is the period for role clarifications. The agency begins to explain to the various potential stakeholders its aims, development approaches and its methodological orientation, the type of groups to be targeted and conditions attached to such partnership.

iii) Situation analysis community diagnosis baseline survey: This is a process that will involve participatory process of needs assessment, identification of local resources, opportunities and constraints, as well as understanding causes of various problems. Participatory Rural Appraisal (PRA) has been found to be an effective approach at this stage of community entry and mobilization.

iv) Target group selection: The idea is to avoid the possibility of 'hijacking' of resources meant for poor by the rich and those in power. There are various wealth ranking techniques for the purpose, as long as one takes care not to offend the people by overlooking their cultural meaning and understanding of the poor and the rich.

v) Deciding on the action to be taken/implemented: Communities are helped to plan for action to transform their situation. The process of PRA should to community Action plans (CAP)based on felt needs and priorities from bottom-up. Implementation of such plans should, as possible, be a local responsibility.

vi) Training for sustainability and maintenance: Capacity building will form part of the agency's plans towards sustainability. Relevant technical skills will be imparted to the local resource people including project management and community organization skills. Care should be taken to avoid creating knowledge and skills monopoly resulting from concentrating training on few selected personalities. This is overcome by insisting on fair distribution of training opportunities among the people. Training teams are recommended as opposed to individuals from a project or region. Needs are prioritized accordingly.

vii) Participatory monitoring and evaluation and sharing of benefits or losses: Local people will have to monitor and evaluate their efforts as a learning process. They should also learn to appreciate the need to share the outcome of their efforts equitably whether such outcome is positive (gain) or negative (loss). It should be remembered that not all gains or losses are tangible. Some are intangible (or abstract) such as fame and reputation emanating from a successful. Community endeavor. Similarly, loss that needs to be shared equitably could be intangible such as blame and ridicule from unsuccessful initiatives that are said to have drained community resources. In such cases, the entire group or community should take responsibility for the results instead of apportioning blame entirely on the leaders for the turn of events.

viii) Local organization formation and strengthening: Community organizations are expected to take over and fill- in the role of external agencies towards sustainability. These organizations should be made up of the target groups themselves through their representatives.

ix) **Withdrawal:** A gradual phasing out of the external agency's support in both human financial resources is imperative. After withdrawal, some minimum external guidance may be provided as may be necessary, but on a more or less consultative basis. The withdrawing external change agents may visit the communities from time to time to encourage as well as learn from their efforts and progress.

x) **Documentation:** It is advisable to document project experience for the record and as lessons to those who may wish to work in the area in future. Such lessons are also bound to inform similar initiatives and replication elsewhere.

4.6 Challenges of Community Mobilization

Some of the commonly cited challenges that tend to negatively affect the effectiveness of development workers within a frozen community include: -

- Negative community attitudes towards new innovations and new ideas. People realize that they have lived with problems long enough to know how to cope. Any new possibilities tend to appear threatening as they will change the existing traditions and disturb the comfort of status quo

- Outsiders are accepted but often with suspicion over their purpose. Are the strangers honest in their concern about our fate? What is the outsiders 'interest? What are they likely to benefit by assisting us? Open dialogue should be used to address these genuine questions. Creating of a good relationship and trust is the biggest task.

- Presence of corrupt leaders who are out for personal gain. This curtails community entry for outside development agents. In such a situation you have to uphold diplomacy tilla time when enough awareness has been created and then tell corrupt leaders off or substitute them completely.

- Apathy: Persons overall belief that something cannot change and their destiny cannot be altered because it is determined. Persons resigning from responsibility due to life challenging and instead laying their blame on supernatural powers, witchcraft or fate. This leads to hatred of neighbors who seem to lead better lives.

- Poor knowledge among the majority. This is in regard to the social dynamics of manipulation in their societies. People may also be exploited because of their docileness and eventually not being in a position to realize that they were being exploited. Creating awareness and lobbying activities releases person's critical faculties and lets their eyes open to reality. The action is expected to be led by this.

- Inability to empathize with the community situation without sympathizing. To empathize is to identify with the community suffering while to sympathize is to cry with them. The latter is not desirable. The change agent should instead remain the source of hope and encouragement.

- Local elite often seek to "own" the change agents. To avoid this keep one's distance but maintain diplomacy with the elite. One should work more closely with the emergent leadership. Through experience it is wiser to seek disengagement from the elite and legitimizers quickly as possible, after community has acknowledged the presence of agents. There is a believe that elite and legitimizers always tend to blind outsiders by denying them to get the full picture of local reality. Usually elite have interests of protecting for themselves or by proxy.

- Perpetration or the creation of community dependency on donors. The agent of change should make it clear from the beginning, that the relationship has a time frame and work out with the people the phase-over plans as early as possible. By creating new change agents from within community as quickly as possible will withstand the external change agent's roles. It is important to make it a policy not to do for the people what they can do for themselves. One should seek to break the tradition of dependency. Many communities continuously suffer because of too much dependency on government and those working in the city to initiate development in the rural areas. It is also necessary to ensure that people elect leaders from the community members as opposed to electing those who live away from them.

4.7 Needs Assessment

When collecting information on needs of a community, it is important to identify the most appropriate approach. Needs assessment is commonly done through the use of a survey. A survey is a data collection tool used to collect data concerning individuals. Surveys may be used to get self-report information from community members. A survey might emphasize on individuals factual data or opinions of community members. There are two main types of surveys that are conducted within communities:

1. Non-formal listening survey.
In this approach, the agent of change lives within the community and participates in their activities. Through such interaction, the agent to change gets an opportunity to record peoples' concerns without interviewing them. This is a very effective way of getting the deepest feelings of a community. Listening helps identify the issues that touch the community. The agent of change should listen with the intention of understanding that people are: hopeful, fearful, concerned, happy or unhappy about. It is not possible to get this kind of information through an interview. Listening is therefore very important.

2. Formal Survey
This is the type of study that involves interviews or administration of questionnaires. Survey for needs assessment should be carried out by professionals. The survey team should consist of people who have some understanding of social psychology, that is, people who have knowledge of how people think, their responses or their general interactive behavior. They should be conversant with adult education, local culture and language. It is important to include some popular members of the community in the survey team. This is likely to influence the success of such survey. If the survey is through interview, one must explain the

objective in a language that the community understands. It is also important to explain the fact that the survey includes everybody to make sure that the clients feel at ease. Sensitive data should be collected by acceptable, and mature people. Professionals prefer being interviewed by other professionals.

4.8 Needs Prioritization

After assessing the needs that exist in a community, it is necessary to do needs' prioritization; that is to arrange needs in order of importance and urgency. Needs could be broadly classified as biogenic and sociogenic.

Maslow came up with 5 levels of needs which were hierarchical in importance which means that the lower ones must be addressed before those in higher levels. When humans are satisfied with physiological needs, they focus on their safety. Lack of safety brings about pre-occupation with fear. Once the individual is secure, he or she focuses on the need for social belonging. When one feels accepted in the social environment, the need for recognition and own dignity (self-esteem) emerges. One seeks for recognition. When this is realized, individuals pursue what they could optimally be in life.

When prioritizing the needs of a community, effectiveness is achieved when community members participate in the identification of their most urgent needs. To ensure this, the agent of change should ensure the community members discuss the problems among themselves. At the stage of prioritization, the agent of change helps them identify their strengths and helps identify the available resources in the community. Such resources include skills that individual members have and what is available within a community. The agent of change should involve the community members in every decision made i.e. the bottom –up approach should be used.

Furthermore, the agent of change should identify with the traditions of the community that he or she is working with. This increases one's acceptability. It is wrong to blatantly condemn the practices of any community and it is the duty of an agent of change to show appreciation of the people's way of life. Community members are usually proud of their way of life since they have always existed within their traditions. When community members learn that they are appreciated, they become cooperative. Any signs of contempt, especially at the entry point, lead to failure since it is not easy to convince the members to listen to the agent of change no matter how much the subsequent effort.

References

Addiction Research Foundation (1986). A Training Program on Prevention in the Drug Field. Toronto. Bacon,

Marjorie, et al. The Volunteers Manual. Toronto: Nell Warren Associates.

Black, Rob. (February 1992). Taking Your Organization's Pulse. Factsheet: Ontario Ministry of Agriculture and Food. Order No. 94-005

Bokor, Chuck (Reprinted 1994). Procedures for Meetings. Factsheet: Ontario Ministry of Agriculture and Food. Order No. 94-003

Bokor, Chuck (Reprinted February, 1995). Working with Volunteers. Factsheet: Ontario Ministry of Agriculture and Food. Order No. 87-012

Bracht, Neil and Agis Tsouros (1990). Principles and strategies of effective community participation.

Health Promotion International 5:3, 199-208.

British Columbia Ministry of Health (1989). Develop goals and objectives. In Healthy Communities: The Process: 22.

Busuttil, Linda et al (1992). Circles of Change: A Process for Animating Rural Communities. Guelph, Ontario:

School of Rural Planning and Development, University of Guelph.

Byvelds, Rita and Joanne Newman (Reprinted January 1992). Understanding Change. Factsheet. Ontario

Ministry of Agriculture and Food. Order No. 91-014

Canadian Centre for Philanthropy. Foundation Proposal Writing Workshop. Toronto

Clark, V. and Simpson, K (Reprinted July 1994). Strategic Planning . . . Is It for You? Ontario Ministry of Agriculture and Food. Order No. 93-041

CUSO (1987). Planning a public meeting. In How To Do It: A Program Planning Guide For Development Education (pp. 19-20).

CUSO (1992). Here to Stay: A Resource Kit on Environmentally Sustainable Development.

Dupont, Jean-Marc and Ken Hoffman (1992). Community Health Centres and Community Development.

Ottawa: Health Services and Promotion Branch, Health and Welfare Canada.

Fleming, Peter (Reprinted February 1995). Strategic Planning. Ontario Ministry of Agriculture and Food, November 1989. Order No. 89-173

Frame, J. Davidson (1987). Managing Projects in Organizations. San Francisco: Jossey-Bass Publishers. Gastil, J.

(1993). Democracy in Small Groups: Participation, Decision Making & Communication. Philadelphia: New Society Publishers.

The Healthcare Forum (1993). Mastering change. In Healthier Communities Action Kit: A Guide for Leaders Embracing Change (pp.64-68). San Francisco.

Hutchison, B. (1993). Assessing community. Health Promotion Summer School on Community Development (pp. 4-11). September 16-October 1, 1993.

Larmer, Nancy (Reprinted July 1994). Recruiting Volunteers. Factsheet: Ontario Ministry of Agriculture and Food. Order No.89-176

London Community Resource Centre (1996). Roles and Responsibilities of Boards of Directors of Non-Profit Organizations. London, Ontario

London Community Resource Centre (1999). Guide to Funding Sources for Non-Profit Organizations. London, Ontario.

MacLeod, Flora (1993). Motivating and Managing Today's Volunteers. N. Vancouver: Self-Counsel Press.

McDowell, Judith Alldritt and Associates. (1992). The 1992 Healthy Communities Yearbook. Victoria,

B.C.: Office of Health Promotion, Ministry of Health and Ministry Responsible for Seniors.

McKnight, J. and Kretzmann, J. (1993). Building communities from the inside out: a path towards finding and mobilizing community assets. Chicago: Centre for Urban Affairs and PolicyResearch

McNair, D. (1989). Strategic Planning for Development Educators. Port Alberni, B.C.: Canadian Council for International Co-operation.

Mitiguy, Nancy (1978). Checklist for reviewing proposals. In The Rich Get Richer and The Poor Write Proposals. Massachusetts: University of Massachusetts.

Muegge, Jane and Nancy Ross (Reprinted July 1994). Volunteers: The Heart of Community Organizations.

Factsheet. Ontario Ministry of Agriculture and Food. Order No. 92-039.   Nell   Warren Associates, Inc. (1991). The Workshops Manual.

North Island Women's Services Society (1984). Working Collectively. Campbell River, B.C.: Ptarmigan Press Ltd.

Ontario Healthy Communities Coalition (2001). Strategies for Effective Proposal-Writing. Toronto, Ontario.

Ontario Ministry of Agriculture, Food and Rural Affairs. Community checklist (handout). In Rural Community Development. Strengthening Rural Communities.

Ontario Premier's Council on Health, Well-being and Social Justice (1994). Why must we change? In Yours,

Mine and Ours: Ontario's Children and Youth (pp.16-19). Toronto: Queen's Printer for Ontario.

Ontario Prevention Clearinghouse (1994). Congress keynotes sound warnings about change. The Ontario Prevention Clearinghouse Newsletter 5:1, 1-2.

Ontario Prevention Clearinghouse (November 1991). Funding Strategies for Health Promotion Resource Package. Toronto, Ontario.

Peterborough Healthy Communities Network (1992). Proceedings from the Peterborough Healthy Communities Network, May 1st, 1992 Session.

Piette, Danielle (1990). Community participation in formal decision-making mechanisms. Health Promotion International 5:3:187-197.

The Public Interest Research Group (February, 1994). The Public Interest Research Group Working Group Guide Quick, Thomas L. (1992). Group problem solving and decision making. In Successful Team Building. New York: Amacom.

Rowan, Elaine, Laura Torrible, and Sandy Turner. Green Communities: A Guide to Taking Action. Toronto: The Conservation Council of Ontario.

Shields, Katrina (1994). In the Tiger's Mouth: An Empowerment Guide for Social Action. Philadelphia, PA: New Society Publishers.

Strategic Planning for Community Development: Winning Through Participation. Toronto: PEOPLE energy and The Canadian Institute of Cultural Affairs.

Sullivan, Terry. (1991). Strategic planning for health: how to stay on top of the game. Health Promotion 30:1: 210.

Underwood, Amber (Reprinted November 1987). Effective Meetings. Factsheet. Ontario Ministry of Agriculture and Food. Order No. 87-011.

www.ingramcontent.com/pod-product-compliance
Lightning Source LLC
Chambersburg PA
CBHW030557220526
45463CB00007B/3104